LIVING A
PURPOSEFUL
Retirement

LIVING A
PURPOSEFUL
Retirement

Bring Happiness and Meaning
to Your Retirement

HYRUM W. SMITH

mango
PUBLISHING GROUP

CORAL GABLES

Conceived, compiled, and edited by Annie Oswald and Natasha Vera
Cover, Layout & Design: Roberto Núñez
Illustrations: Marina Zlochin/Adobe Stock

For permission requests, please contact the publisher at:
Mango Publishing Group
2850 S Douglas Road, 2nd Floor
Coral Gables, FL 33134 USA
info@mango.bz

For special orders, quantity sales, course adoptions and corporate sales,
please email the publisher at sales@mango.bz. For trade and wholesale
sales, please contact Ingram Publisher Services at customer.service@
ingramcontent.com or +1.800.509.4887.

Living a Purposeful Retirement: Bring Happiness and Meaning to
Your Retirement

Library of Congress Cataloging-in-Publication number: #######
ISBN: (print) 978-1-64250-507-8, (ebook) ###-#-#####-###-#
BISAC category code BUS050040—BUSINESS & ECONOMICS /
Personal Finance / Retirement Planning

Printed in the United States of America

TABLE OF CONTENTS

INTRODUCTION

Retirement can be a gift—a gift that opens up right in front of us like a perfect parking spot. It's a gift of time and a gift of opportunity. But we must first recognize it.

Nowadays, the word retirement has a somewhat negative connotation because it is associated with being the end of something. In this case, the end of a significant and lifelong journey.

"It's ridiculous!" you might say.

Then don't stop. Don't let it be your "end."

Take this gift of time. Take this gift of opportunity. Take this gift and redirect your life. Take this gift and purposefully redirect your retirement.

You've left your day job and perhaps even turned off your alarm clock. But that doesn't mean it's time to grab a crocheted blanket, wear down your favorite recliner, and start shouting out "What is" answers at re-runs of Alex Trebek.

I'm surely not going to let someone hand me a Social Security check and shoo me away. I am going to treat retirement as *my time.* I am going to ensure I make a difference with the time I am given.

In my seventies, I would be the first to tell you I didn't traditionally "retire." I just started doing something else. I just changed my daily scenery. Now it's time for you to do the same!

Part 1

REVITALIZE

Reframing Your Mind for the
Exciting Possibilities Ahead

The purpose of this book is to get you thinking
about the many options for this new exciting phase
of your life and to inspire you to make it purposeful.
It's your chance to make a difference in your life,
the lives of those around you, and even the world.

Retirees all around you are living longer.
And living better! Retirement is no longer an
end. It's a *new season* to live purposefully.

Don't "retire"! Instead, join me in doing something else. Take note of the advice and inspiration here that rings true to you. Take away some ideas. Make plans today. Because you're not done and you're definitely not dead yet!

"You don't stop laughing when you grow old, you grow old when you stop laughing."

—GEORGE BERNARD SHAW

Retirement is YOUR time.
Make a difference with it!

You are valuable not
because of your job title, but
because of who you are.

Retirement is a gift. It's
a gift of time and a gift
of opportunities.

You're not defined by your job, your title,
or the size of your paycheck. Ask yourself
this: "When it is gone, what is left?"

We each have a "Belief Window" through which we look and perceive our lives. This window contains all our perceptions of the world. It shows us what we think we know. The view from everyone's Belief Window is different based on upbringing, environment, and life experiences.

As you see your world through your Belief Window, it affects every thought of every day. And if you can change your principles on your Belief Window, you can change your life.

"Age is an issue of mind over matter. If you don't mind, it doesn't matter."

—MARK TWAIN

What can you do with this gift of time?

- Launch a new career—the one you always wanted to do but couldn't because you needed a predictable paycheck.

- Volunteer and make a difference in your community.

- Focus on spending time with your family.

- Fulfill your dream of being a DJ.

- Write a novel.

- Be a greeter and have an excuse to talk to people all day long.

- Take tickets at a movie theater or help people find their seats.

- Go on adventures with your partner.

- Ride bicycles with your grandkids.

- Try something you have never done before.

Now is the time to consider all options, because now you finally have the time to do so!

"Change can be a good thing, and that is what retirement is—a really big change."

—ANN BARNES

Take this gift of time and choose to do so much more.

Part 2

THINK, DREAM, VISUALIZE, PLAN

Planning, Time Management,
and Practical Advice

The best litmus test for productivity is to ask yourself, "What did I do today? What did I accomplish today?" If you find yourself floundering, set your intentions for the day, the week, the month, the year, ahead of time to give you a read map for how you want to spend your time, set your intentions now for the day, the week, the month, the year.

Daily planning gives you a *shield* against being lost in busy-ness. It takes you out of the busy world and into the *productivity* world.

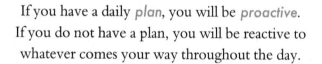

If you have a daily *plan*, you will be *proactive*.
If you do not have a plan, you will be reactive to
whatever comes your way throughout the day.

The option is clear, either you can consciously
plan and decide how you want to fill your time
and act purposefully or you can allow outside
forces to fill time for you. In the river of life,
be a boat you steer, not a log that drifts.

Go beyond asking yourself: *What am I going to do today? What am I going to do this week?* Go deeper and ask: *How am I going to make a difference?*

"Retirement is not for me. It's for the people I can serve. It's for the friends and family I can help and the younger generation I can teach."

—BJ GALLAGHER

If you understand your values, your inner self, you have unleashed a driving force in your own personal path to form a purposeful retirement. You know what you value, and therefore you know where you should direct your time, your energy, and your resources.

These three steps—*identify*, *clarify*, and *prioritize*—illuminate your priorities. Now the challenge is to build a retirement that reflects these values.

Develop a personal constitution. Once you do that, you will absolutely know what you want to do in this season of your life.

The clock tells you nothing about time. Time is the occurrence of events in sequence one after the other. If that is true, the only things I can control about time are the events in my life.

There is no hierarchy of choices. What does matter is that you choose to do something.

Choose to do something that will give you a reason to get out of bed in the morning.

Choose to do something that will put some space between you and the recliner.

Choose to do something that will give you purpose to your retirement. Choose to live a purposeful retirement.

*"We make a living by what we get,
but we make a life by what we give."*

—WINSTON CHURCHILL

Periodically stop and ask yourself,
"Have you made a difference?"

Quite a lot has been said about the role retirees can play as mentors. Have you considered the fact that *you* need a *mentor* in your own retirement?

Look around and find someone you admire,
someone who has already retired. Ask what they
like about retirement. What do they recommend
doing? What do they wish they had done
differently in retirement, right from the start?

Picture what you want. Say in your mind or even out loud: "I want my retirement to look like..."

Now that you have retired, set aside the fear and duty. Plan to do what you love to do. When we act out of love, miracles happen. What do you love to do?

You do not need to rely on previous accomplishments. You can spin *new stories*. You can write new tales.

Remember what you loved most
about your last day job and find a way
to make it fit into your new life.

Are you ready to volunteer? It's easy! Find a local community theater and volunteer as an usher. Provide rides to the hospital or to the grocery store for someone in need. Play music or sing at a retirement center. Mow your neighbor's lawn. Repair someone's car.

"There is a fountain of youth: It is your mind, your talents, the creativity you bring to your life and the lives of people you love. When you learn to tap this source, you will truly have defeated age."

—SOPHIA LOREN

The important thing is to choose what makes
you feel joy and satisfaction, what makes you
feel like you are making a difference, and what
will help you be happy in your retirement.

We need to stop talking about the younger
generation as though we had nothing
to do with creating it. We need to stop
judging and model better behavior. And
we need to start with ourselves.

Whatever you choose to do, make it a priority. Take care of your brain. Go to an art museum and read the pamphlet on the artist. Read the book before you watch the movie. Keep your brain sharp and active.

"When things are a challenge, I like to take them on. I just hit it, head-on. I don't let myself be afraid."

—GAIL SMITH

Everyone has their dream retirement.
The difficulty is being brave enough to
make that dream come true, whether it's
fishing every day or seeing the world.

In retirement, I *commit* to being fully present to the people around me and ask others to do the same. When my grandkids enter my home, they know they need to put all devices in a basket by the door.

Make an appointment with your partner. Sit down with each other. Talk. No cell phones, no iPads, just talking and planning together on a regular, scheduled basis. Be present with each other.

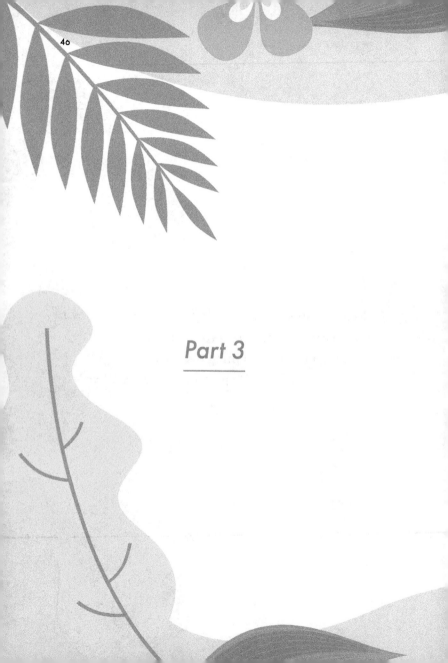

Part 3

A PURPOSEFUL
NEW BEGINNING

Motivation, Calls to Action, and
Ideas for a Purposeful Retirement

Go ahead and ask yourself: "What would I really like to do? When am I going to do it?" Go ahead! Write your answers right here on the page!

The marriage you have before retirement is the marriage you will have after retirement, only amplified. In your retirement, you will reap what you have sown during your partnership.

It's never too late to start *positive* interactions. This can also be a time for a fresh start!

Talk about how to divide things so one partner is not unfairly burdened. If you do not retire at the same time, the partner who has been home the longest may look forward to help. It's time for a new negotiation.

When figuring out the new normal of
both partners being at home, try these
negotiation techniques with your partner:

Choose a good time to talk. If there is a decision
to be made, try not to talk about it in times of
stress. Give each other your full attention.

Remove all distractions. Thoroughly discuss
all options and perspectives. Never give up
and say "I don't care" if you do indeed care.

Choose a solution that works for both of you.

It's a *new* beginning. Talk with one another and find a new routine that makes you both happy. As you *adjust*, remember to have expectations for yourself, but not expectations for your partner.

Relationships need to be nurtured before
retirement so that when you are together
all day long, the idea makes you happy,
instead of panicked and depressed.

No matter how great your marriage is, there can be such a thing as too much time together. Encourage your spouse to meet up with friends. Send them out on activities and lunches. Do not hold each other back. You'll both be happier for it.

Do not allow loneliness to become a part of your retirement. It won't let you go. It's unhealthy, and sometimes it's deadly.

If you feel loneliness creeping up on you,
here are some ideas on how to reach
out and keep loneliness at bay:

- Make new friends.
- Go "clubbing" (book club,
  bridge club, walking club).
- Babysit the newest members of your family.
- Volunteer with an organization
  you're passionate about.

The greatest friendships are formed as we serve
one another and with one another. When
you are involved in making a difference, you
form friendships with the people serving right
alongside you. Making friends is a natural
byproduct of service and making a difference.

Do not worry about making friends. Worry about being *kind*. Worry about being *loyal*. Worry about *helping* others. And your friend pool will begin to fill in.

Did you know that Bram Stoker didn't write *Dracula* until he was fifty? Laura Ingalls Wilder was in her mid-sixties when she finally published *Little House in the Big Wood*s. Anna Sewell published *Black Beauty* when she was fifty-seven. Delia Owens published her bestseller *Where the Crawdads Sing* when she was almost seventy.

We tend to think a legacy needs to be something worthy of the front page of the newspaper. Living an honest life is a legacy.

Share your story. *Sharing* is learning. It is something of great value we can give to those we love. Keep communicating.

If you want to keep your brain functioning at
a high level, new research tells us to babysit,
at least in moderation. Spending time with
our grandchildren keeps us young.

If you want to communicate better and develop stronger relationships, communicate both your way and their way. Your way may be a phone call or handwritten letter whereas theirs might be texting, tweeting, or getting on other social media.

What a wonderful *gift* you give when you spend
time communicating with your grandchildren!
It will be a gift that goes both ways.

Welcome to the state of downsizing, when you realize that more stuff just means more things to dust and clean. Unload some of those knickknacks!

Clean up yourself as well as your home!
Can you eat *better*? Can you make
healthier choices? Can you set the stage
for a *happier* and healthier retirement?

Keep a *positive* attitude. We all know people who only want to talk about their bad health. They want to talk about every single ache in every single bone. Don't do that! Instead, focus on what parts of your body *feel good!*

When your friends start complaining, change the topic! Talk about what you're reading. Talk about what you saw on your walk around the block. Talk about the next vacation you are planning. Talk about anything else.

Physical activity stimulates endorphins,
natural chemicals which promote a physical
feeling of happiness. If you are looking
for more happiness in your life, look for
more ways to incorporate *exercise*.

Practice "Habit 2: Begin with the End in Mind," from *The 7 Habits of Highly Effective People*. Visualize your ultimate goal and then put it in writing.

We all experience physical limitations
at different times. Be wise, but be
committed to an *active* lifestyle.

Control your own *future* by
making decisions today.

No one wants to be a burden to their family. Recognize that you won't always be able to do the things you now can do. Face the fear so you can make a plan to overcome it.

What are you willing to do to experience a purposeful retirement? What expectations do you have for yourself? How are you scripting your second act?

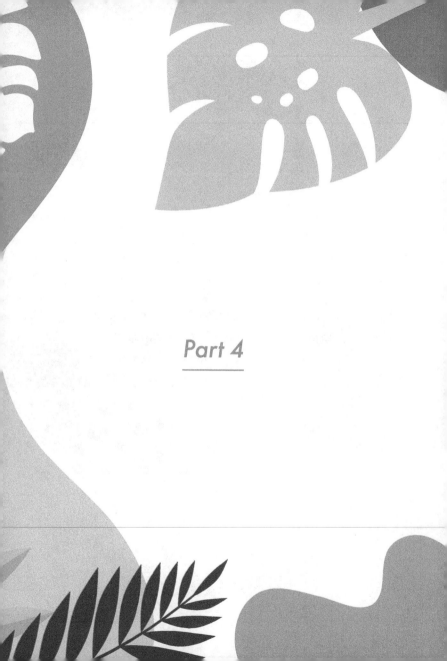

Part 4

MAKE YOUR MARK!

Leaving Your Legacy

Welcome to your second act! It's yours to plan as you desire. What do you want to be? What do you want to do? Now is the time to create a new season—a purposeful retirement.

Every season of change gives you an opportunity to decide who you want to be. You can take the good, leave the bad, and decide who you want to be and what you want to do going forward.

"I slept and dreamt that life was joy. I awoke and saw that life was service. I acted and behold, service was joy."

—RABINDRANATH TAGORE, BENGALI POET AND ARTIST

The key is to act and to choose to find joy.

Whoever you were before you retired, chances are that's who you are today. But don't despair if it's not who you want to be. There is plenty of time for change. Start now!

This era of time is called "the freedom zone." It's the state where we enjoy the greatest balance of *freedom*, health, free time, and emotional well-being.

Being happy—finding joy—is simple. It's just not *easy*. You have to work for it. There is no substitute for work at any point in your life, even in retirement. There is a price to be paid, and that price is your time and your dedication to ensuring that it happens.

In retirement, you have to shift your
definition of success. Personally, I have
always defined success like this: a successful
person is willing to do those things that
unsuccessful people are not willing to do.

What is the source of your *happiness*? Only you can answer that question. But it's guaranteed: being bored is not anyone's source of happiness.

What makes you happy? Is it...

- Reading a book?
- Having lunch with a child or grandchild?
- Volunteering at a local theater or school?
- Golfing with a friend?
- Gardening and growing your own food?
- Traveling and having new experiences?
- Spending time with your dog?
- Cooking and discovering new recipes?

My wife, Gail, looks at retirement as a continuation of life's adventure. Retirement is a time to do new things. It's a different time, a different season. When you fall into that season, you can learn to love it.

In retirement, you mostly get to choose your own stress. Life in retirement is not going to be perfect. There are still things you have to deal with. But now you're in charge of your own time.

You are no longer compelled by a job and its responsibilities. While you are in control, while you are making choices, why not choose to be happy?

"They say a person needs just three things to be truly happy in this world: someone to love, something to do, and something to hope for."

—TOM BODETT, AUTHOR AND RADIO BROADCASTER

Now is the perfect time to take stock of where you have been, what you have done, and what you want to do in the future. Now is the time to acknowledge mistakes and decide how you want to act differently going forward. Now is the time to choose happiness.

Purposeful Planning Questions

1. What makes you happy?
   When do you feel joy?

2. How can you incorporate more joy
   into your purposeful retirement?

3. What can you do right now to find more joy?

Ask yourself: What are other happy and successful
retirees doing? Am I willing to do that?

CONCLUSION

Most of us spend around fifty years of our lives working, and no matter your occupation, your working life is deeply encoded in your identity. It is not so easy to simply drop this side of you as you enter a new phase of your life. The best advice I can pass along is that you are still you. You bring the same value to the world even when you stop going to work five days a week. In fact, you might be able to contribute *more* in service to the world by giving back to others, a marvelous benefit that comes with the opportunity to manage your time in a different way.

It's all in your hands, completely up to you. You have a choice, and my suggestion is that you embrace these years with zest. Whatever you do, do not withdraw from life or sit around and wait for things to happen. Be passionate, not passive.

The rest of your life can be the best of your life. Each day is a gift and an opportunity to improve your relationships, stimulate your mind, invigorate your body, and grow spiritually. Retirement can easily provide an unbelievably bright future for you and your loved ones. You are not a "has been," you are a "will be." Above all, be purposeful. Enjoy the gift of retirement. Enjoy all that lies before you!

ABOUT THE AUTHOR

The late Hyrum W. Smith was one of the original creators of
the popular Franklin Day Planner and the recognized "Father
of Time Management." Hyrum was the former Chairman and
CEO of FranklinCovey Co. He served as Vice-Chairman of
the Board of Tuacahn Center for the Arts.

For over four decades, Hyrum empowered people to
effectively govern their personal and professional lives. This
distinguished author, speaker, and businessman combined wit
and enthusiasm with a gift for communicating compelling
principles that incite lasting personal change.

Hyrum authored nationally-acclaimed books and
presentations including *The 10 Natural Laws of Successful Time
and Life Management*; *What Matters Most*; *Pain is Inevitable,
Misery is Optional*; *You Are What You Believe*; *The Three Gaps;*
and *Purposeful Retirement*.

Hyrum passed away in 2019 and is survived by his loving
wife, Gail.

"*It's all in your hands, completely up to you. You have a choice, and my suggestion is that you embrace these years with zest. Whatever you do, do not withdraw from life or sit around and wait for things to happen. Be passionate, not passive. The rest of your life can be the best of your life.*"

—HYRUM SMITH

A TRIBUTE TO HYRUM SMITH

By Boyd Matheson, opinion editor of *Deseret News*

Hyrum was one of the greatest leadership and human development speakers America has ever produced. He was an entrepreneur, author, gifted teacher, philanthropist, and founder of Franklin Quest Company which eventually merged with Stephen R. Covey's company to form Franklin Covey.

I was nineteen years old when my dad handed me a cassette tape with Hyrum W. Smith printed on it. He told me I should listen to it. I put it in the tape recorder and hit play. Hyrum's distinct, penetrating voice boomed from the speakers with an intensity that captured me and a gentleness that invited me to engage. On that day, he was speaking to me. I think I listened to the recording four times before the sun set. I eventually played it so many times it broke.

Even today, I can hear his distinct cadence as he would share his version of the oft recited quote, "There is no chance, no fate, no destiny that can circumvent or hinder or control the firm resolve of a determined soul." Millions around the world could likewise repeat, on command, the principles and nuggets of wisdom from this charismatic, larger-than-life man with a gentle soul.

What a difference that day made for me. It nudged me onto a path in the pursuit of excellence for the next thirty-four years. I have passionately studied and taught the leadership principles I first learned from Hyrum to organizations around the world. Those same principles shaped the way I tried to have influence and lead a Senate staff in our nation's capital, and they continue to impact my approach to sharing principles in my current chair here as opinion editor of the Deseret News and host of the Inside Sources radio program on KSL.

I eventually met Hyrum and had the chance to spend time with him and his amazing wife, Gail, on their ranch in Southern Utah. We stayed up late into the night talking about principles, the things that matter and how to make a difference. The next morning, I watched them get their grandchildren ready for their annual cattle drive. It was like watching a well-choreographed dance conducted by two maestros. Gail warmed up what seemed to be twenty horses. She had the horses circling the corral with a symmetry and pace that was mesmerizing. Meanwhile, Hyrum guided the grandchildren through saddles, bridles, supplies and gear, eventually helping them all saddle up and get ready to ride. Everyone had a job, everyone was responsible for everyone; I didn't hear a single shout, cry, or complaint. It was a lesson in leadership that spanned every level of human interaction. What a day! What a difference for me.

Hyrum W. Smith passed away on November 18, 2019 after a battle with cancer. What a difference a day makes. Hyrum was a presence, a force for good, a difference maker—all of which makes his absence all the harder to accept. But he left a legacy of what he taught and how he lived; he showed how to maximize and make a difference for others with those 1,440 minutes that make up every day.

Mango Publishing, established in 2014, publishes an eclectic list of books by diverse authors—both new and established voices—on topics ranging from business, personal growth, women's empowerment, LGBTQ+ studies, health and spirituality to history, popular culture, time management, decluttering, lifestyle, mental wellness, aging, and sustainable living. We were named 2019 and 2020's #1 fastest growing independent publisher by Publishers Weekly. Our success is driven by our main goal, which is to publish high quality books that will entertain readers as well as make a positive difference in their lives.

Our readers are our most important resource; we value your input, suggestions, and ideas. We'd love to hear from you—after all, we are publishing books for you!

Please stay in touch with us and follow us at:

Facebook: Mango Publishing
Twitter: @MangoPublishing
Instagram: @MangoPublishing
LinkedIn: Mango Publishing
Pinterest: Mango Publishing
Newsletter: MangoPublishinggroup.com

Sign up for our newsletter and receive a free book!

Join us on Mango's journey to reinvent publishing, one book at a time.